Leadership

Enhancing Self-assurance And Cognitive Empathy For
The Purpose Of Cultivating A Productive And
Synergistic Team

*(Achieving Equilibrium Between Rationality And
Emotion)*

Kenneth Ramsay

TABLE OF CONTENT

Trust 1
Leadership Quality 4
Enhancement In Corporates 4
The Science And Craft Of Business Coaching 8
Attain Goals Through Conducting Facilitated Strategy Sessions 22
The Self-Disciplined Leader 37
Exert Positive Influence With Finesse 42
Staff Management Qualities 63
Recognize The Importance Of Your Millennial Workforce And Afford Them Opportunities For Development 80
Please Ensure The Stimulation Of One's Intellect 96
The Phenomenon Of Love 112

Trust

It is exceedingly challenging to effectively guide individuals who lack confidence in your leadership. When an employee places trust in their supervisor, they can maintain assurance that their rights and interests will be safeguarded against any form of exploitation. Maintain transparency and ensure regular communication with individuals. Exhibit forthrightness when discussing issues. Recognize and acknowledge deserving individuals by attributing credit appropriately while maintaining fairness. Avoid appearing aloof and detached, and aim to refrain from exclusively focusing on concrete data. Exhibit unwavering consistency and consistently adhere to honesty. A leader who is discovered to be untruthful encounters significant challenges in regaining trust. You must ensure that you honor your commitments. Exercise utmost discretion in safeguarding the confidences entrusted to you. Individuals require trustworthy leaders who can be entrusted with confidential information. If individuals perceive you as lacking the ability to maintain confidentiality, your credibility within the organization will be compromised. I strongly recommend the literary work The Speed of Trust authored by Stephen M. R. Covey. There are numerous benefits to being seen as trustworthy. It will imbue you with a sense of self-satisfaction. Your reputation will attract the favor and interest of others when it comes to engaging with you. Exhibiting a sense of reliability is an esteemed personal characteristic. It entails embodying qualities such as honesty, dependability, and accountability. Individuals will regard you with greater respect and exhibit a desire to sustain communication with an individual who consistently demonstrates dependability. Throughout my tenure, I have been privileged to bear witness to a myriad of singular narratives conveyed by my subordinates. I have refrained from divulging them to anyone except in instances when it was necessary to do so, such as when sharing them with another individual holding a managerial or human resources position. I divulged the information solely out of concern for the welfare and wellbeing of an employee.

Leadership Quality Enhancement In Corporates

As individuals progress along the trajectory of their professional trajectory, it is imperative for their intrinsic leadership capabilities to become increasingly refined. Therefore, as we progress in our roles as professional leaders, it is imperative that we become familiarized with societal norms, the civil code, ethical practices in business and their impact on humanity, legal viewpoints, and the developmental objectives for emerging leaders. If these attributes are not evident as an individual progresses in their professional career, it may be inferred that they have not developed into a leadership role and their presence could potentially lead to a deterioration of the corporate culture. The reality is that "leaders create leaders," and if an employee lacks the essential qualities and deep comprehension of leadership, despite being mistakenly promoted to a leadership role based on subjective recommendations from corporate management, they will never possess the ability to foster leadership within others. Moreover, this incorrect leadership will inevitably lead to detrimental effects on corporate culture and hinder corporate advancement.

Psychological perspective: Individuals have a natural inclination to wholeheartedly adhere to their authentic leaders. Employees within an organization are likely to acquire respect, professionalism, friendliness, curiosity, and leadership qualities when they subconsciously align their mindset with the demonstrated leadership traits of their superiors. As a result, a corporate environment that fosters a culture of growth is established. However, in the event that a leadership position is assigned (without any clear justification), the individual occupying the position will experience "cognitive dissonance" and thus impede any potential progress. Therefore, the corporation should carefully monitor the holistic progress (including the acquisition of knowledge in relation to societal norms, legal framework, ethical conduct, etc., throughout the course of time) of an employee prior to promoting them to a position of leadership.

BUSINESS INSIGHT: Monitor the progression of employees as they advance in their careers and foster the development of leadership qualities, thereby nurturing the organizational culture with an objective perspective in mind.

The Science And Craft Of Business Coaching

Attainment of prosperity in business often stems from the facilitation of efficient business coaching and astute leadership. Business coaching closely parallels sports coaching. In the realm of sports, the coach motivates and instructs individual members of the team with the objective of achieving victory in competitions. In the realm of business, the coach additionally assumes the responsibility of encouraging, instructing, and guiding their team members towards attaining triumph. "If one desires to enhance their skills as a proficient business coach and leader, the following suggestions can offer valuable assistance:

Engage in professional development programs focused on business coaching

In opposition to prevailing beliefs, the realm of business is characterized by its technical nature, necessitating the pursuit of academic enrollment in a business program to comprehend the intricacies of the discipline in a comprehensive manner. To acquire the necessary skills to excel as a proficient business coach, I would recommend locating a reputable business institution and undertaking the process of admission. This will aid in the refinement of your business coaching abilities.

Have enough business experience

A primary factor contributing to the scarcity of young business coaches is the necessity for significant prior professional expertise in the domain of business coaching. It is advisable to possess prior experience in coaching individuals within the small business sector, as it will provide you with thorough understanding of the challenges and difficulties that both you and your mentee are likely to encounter. Due to the depth of your professional expertise, you will be able to provide highly effective counsel to your clients.

Be supportive

A crucial competency that a proficient business coach must possess is the capacity to deliver assistance and guidance. Given that the objective is to foster the success of clients' businesses, it is imperative that you offer them exhaustive assistance. Reinstate their aspirations and provide them with continuous guidance on the necessary steps to attain them.

Be patient

Not every business you undertake will achieve immediate success. Occasionally, it may require a substantial amount of time for your client's business to achieve success. Hence, a great deal of patience and comprehension is demanded from you, given your role as the acting leader in this specific circumstance.

Be professional

Considering the professional nature of the business domain, it is imperative for you to uphold a demeanor and conduct that is indicative of professionalism. Refrain from personalizing matters and strive to maintain amicable associations not just with clients, but also with fellow professionals in the business realm.

By diligently adhering to the procedures outlined in this chapter, you are bound to become a highly proficient business coach. Ensure that a positive and amicable rapport is maintained with your client. Success will then follow.

Have a vision

Your overall objective exhibits a lucid depiction of your desired destination, yet the route to manifesting this vision is fraught with subordinate objectives and obstacles to surmount. Each objective should serve as a milestone along your journey, and these objectives should be divided into feasible tasks that can be accomplished within a specified time frame.

The possession of a vision may appear somewhat abstract, yet fundamentally, when imparting one's ideas to others, a vision necessitates only two fundamental components. When articulating your vision within a corporate setting, it should be approached akin to a persuasive marketing presentation. However, in this context, your audience comprises higher-ranking colleagues and/or fellow team members, and the objective is to garner their support and endorsement for your concept, rather than promoting tangible goods or services. Your vision should possess the capacity to instill motivation within you and exert a profound influence on others, compelling them to take action. As your visionary aspirations are articulated, an envisaged future unfolds in which collective progress is achieved under your guidance, fostering an equitable and inclusive society.

In addition to the aforementioned primary components, when conveying your vision to others, it is important to ensure that it encompasses responses to the following inquiries:

What are the anticipated accomplishments of you and your team?

Do the values of the vision align?

What long-term impact will it have on you/your team?

What is the estimated duration?

What are the resources required to fulfill your long-term objective?

What specific measures are necessary for achieving success?

By what criteria will success be assessed?

Will the achievement of this success result in detriment or adversity for others?

Does this vision encompass both short-term and long-term solutions?

Basic Outcome Clarification Process

Every scenario is unique and not all principles can be universally applied, however, as a general rule, it is advisable to subject the practicality of your endeavor to an evaluation process in order to ascertain the costs, benefits, and overall viability of the proposed project or task. Prior to the dissemination of your vision, certain fundamental factors warrant careful consideration. It is important to bear in mind that in the realm of business, it is prudent to prioritize pragmatic considerations over idealistic aspirations. This implies that the most advantageous course of action is to pursue profitability, while remaining adaptable in the pursuit of personal dreams.

What impact will the result have on individuals in my vicinity?

Maintain ethical behavior, as individuals strive to avoid causing adverse impacts on their peers. Generally, it can be observed that what is considered optimal for the collective endeavor tends to align with what is deemed beneficial for the individual members involved. I would strongly discourage the prioritization of anything else over the well-being of others, unless it is necessary for the preservation of the business or the team as a whole. Under no circumstances should one jeopardize the safety and welfare of others in pursuit of financial profits.

Can we anticipate whether the result will represent an asset, expense, or liability?

This question bears significant importance and numerous ideas will fail to progress beyond this stage. Although this book does not primarily focus on financial education, it is of utmost significance to classify every project according to its resulting effects in the subsequent manners:

An asset has the potential to generate sustained monetary returns, either through consistent cash flow or by enhancing the value of existing assets, over an extended period of time. Not all assets pertain exclusively to finances; rather, an asset encompasses any element that consistently contributes to or bolsters the success of your business or team.

Typically, an expenditure can be classified in the same category as necessary operational expenses and non-recurring disbursements. Ensure that your expenditures do not masquerade as liabilities. Once you have ascertained that your expenditure is unequivocally an expense, it is crucial to deliberate upon its inherent value and merit. (whatever it may be).

Avoid liabilities. Liabilities incur expenses regularly, be it on a daily, weekly, or monthly basis, yielding minimal or negligible benefits. A prevalent error that individuals often commit is erroneously regarding a car as an asset, while in reality, for certain individuals, a car unequivocally represents a liability that exceeds their financial capacity. Certain individuals may carry this exemplification to an utmost extent by acquiring automobiles via financial means, thereby guaranteeing a perpetual outflow of funds from their financial accounts in the foreseeable period.

Benefits and Costs

When evaluating the advantages of a result, we must once again employ our astuteness. The comprehensive evaluation of advantages versus expenses necessitates considering various interrelated factors.

Financial

Comparing immediate expenses to immediate gains. The comparative analysis of enduring expenses in contrast to enduring advantages. Immediate expenses compared to the enduring advantages.

The consideration of long-term costs in relation to short-term benefits should be wholly disregarded.

Timescale

First and foremost, do I have authority over the timeframe? Would the examination of this outcome result in a postponement of other projects?

Current processes

Any measures implemented or modifications carried out to procedures should uphold the advantages of your current actions. Compromising efficacy in one domain in order to enhance another will necessitate revisiting the initial issue at a later point in time. If the remedy for one predicament engenders another, it implies a flaw within your proposed solution. It is imperative that you revisit the initial stage of generating ideas.

Be Smarterr

Please ensure that you mentally retain the acronym, SMARTERR, as it serves as a useful tool for recalling the core principles of outcome clarification. Does your objective possess attributes such as specificity, measurability, achievability, and relevance within a defined timeframe? After attaining a particular result, it is imperative to conduct an assessment and make necessary modifications, ultimately ensuring the replication of its accomplishments.

Attain Goals Through Conducting Facilitated Strategy Sessions

The primary obligations of leaders in both for-profit and not-for-profit organizations are to effectively allure and retain customers, while ensuring the organization maintains competitiveness within the marketplace. Enterprise operations are sustained by income, irrespective of their tax categorization. At regular intervals ranging from three to five years, astute leaders undertake an evaluative process encompassing various elements, including the organization's existing conditions, the encompassing operational environment, the clientele served, the manner in which products and services are delivered, the prevailing competitive landscape, potential hindrances and risks, as well as visible prospects. It is through the comprehensive analysis of this information that they discern, and subsequently prioritize, objectives that will pave the way for the organization's long-term viability.

It is of utmost importance to establish the optimal conditions for a fruitful strategy planning or process improvement retreat/meeting. The global landscape has undergone a transformation, leaving us with little opportunity to spare on potentially unfruitful "brainstorming sessions" that may have sufficed in previous times. It is highly probable that the outcomes of the planning retreat hold great significance for the organization, and it would be imprudent to let chance or internal political factors dictate the results.

By enlisting the services of a knowledgeable meeting facilitator, one can ensure that the strategy planning or improvement process retreat is conducted with utmost professionalism. This approach will enable participants to effectively identify goals and objectives that adhere to the principles of being SMART (Specific, Measurable, Attainable, Relevant, and Timely), while also gaining the buy-in and support of mid-level managers and other critical members of staff. A facilitator enables the inclusive participation of all stakeholders in the meeting, rather than restricting a pivotal decision-maker to the position of meeting supervisor and time observer.

The facilitator establishes a constructive meeting ambiance conducive to collaboration and efficiency. He/she effectively maintains the participants' attention on the subject matter and ensures a smooth and continuous flow of discussions. In the event that a dominant individual endeavors to seize control of the proceedings, or if the discussion happens to veer off course, the facilitator employs strategies to regain the necessary concentration without causing offense or stifling the active involvement and innovative thinking of the participants.

An adept facilitator possesses the ability to elicit the collective wisdom present amongst the participants. S/he acknowledges that the majority of leaders possess the solutions to the issues encountered by their organization as they have assumed the role of leadership within it. They only need the right flow of energy to bring wisdom and good ideas to the surface. In the event that the group encounters difficulties, the facilitator will assist participants in contemplating the appropriate inquiries that need to be raised, thus providing an alternate avenue for arriving at the correct solutions.

Your meeting facilitator possesses a noteworthy skill in fostering agreement on shared objectives and priorities, even in situations where different perspectives and understanding exist. Assisting conflicting factions in actively engaging with and comprehending the rationale behind the concerns and decisions of the opposing party can foster the identification of a "third way" or a middle ground. This middle ground entails alternatives that encompass the significant merits of both perspectives, acknowledge their respective priorities, and enable the collective to unite around this innovative amalgamation.

Organization leaders demonstrate their commitment to effective stewardship by devising strategies to increase market share, address business obstacles, enhance service delivery and process systems, leverage competitive advantages, and optimize profitability in the next three to five years. Engaging the services of a qualified meeting and strategy planning facilitator ensures that leaders will fulfill these responsibilities and handle them appropriately.

Goal Setting Strategies Employed by Effective Leaders

Leaders must be goal-oriented. Simultaneously, they must possess the capability to execute the necessary actions in order to achieve their objectives. This chapter aims to demonstrate the procedure.

We will employ a straightforward four-part model that can be readily replicated. Each facet holds utmost significance in determining your efficacy as a leader. It is of utmost importance that you diligently adhere to all mandated components without any omissions.

Regard yourself as a constructor. Omitting one of the steps in this approach is tantamount to constructing it without a solid groundwork.

Phase 1: Establishing objectives

The initial phase involves establishing your objectives. These objectives may encompass either short-term or long-term timeframes. These can also be categorized based on timing intervals, such as on a daily, weekly, monthly, and so forth basis.

Regardless of the circumstances, it is advisable to sit down and make incremental progress. The essential skill that you must possess is the art of strategic foresight, as discussed in the preceding section. Since it is imperative to establish objectives in order to meet the expectations and projections of your organization.

As an illustration, may I inquire about your projected annual sales objective? Subsequently, you have the option to categorize them based on monthly, weekly, or daily intervals. These objectives are commonly referred to as 'specific aims.'

This is a component of what is commonly referred to as formulating goals that are Specific, Measurable, Achievable, Relevant, and Time-bound (SMART goals). The acronym SMART is an abbreviation that stands for the following:

Precise: Could you please outline your precise set of objectives? Particular: Kindly elaborate on your particular objectives. Explicit: Please provide

explicit details on your objectives.
Defined: Can you clarify your defined objectives?

How do you plan to gauge your level of achievement? What metrics do you plan to utilize in order to make necessary modifications?

Attainable: By what means will you achieve these objectives? Which measures will you need to undertake to achieve them? What is your method of transportation in order to travel between point A and point B? Whom would be the most suitable individuals to assist you in achieving your objectives?

Significance: What is the importance of this matter to your organization?

Regarding a fixed timeframe: What is the anticipated duration for accomplishing both the primary and secondary objectives?

It is imperative that you respond to these inquiries each time you set a goal. If you are able to accomplish this, you will acquire a comprehensive comprehension of their nature, thereby enabling you to conveniently monitor and manage all relevant data.

It is imperative to comprehend the objective of your organization as well. Why does it exist? What is its purpose?

Phase 2: Formulate your strategic approach

You have successfully outlined your goals. What is your strategy for overcoming them? In order to achieve this objective, it is necessary to carry out an evaluation.

To be more specific, you aspire to gain an understanding of the envisioned outcome once your objectives have been achieved. Subsequently, establish a framework to oversee said objectives and diligently record the pertinent metrics. Shifting our focus back to the sales illustration, it may be imperative to prioritize the volume of units sold alongside the magnitude of revenue generated within a designated timeframe.

You ought to also take into account the potential challenges that may be encountered in the future. What obstacles do you anticipate encountering during your work and how do you plan to overcome them? What is your strategy for overcoming them?

Additionally, it is imperative to establish distinct milestones for each objective that they have successfully achieved. If your monthly sales target is set at 1000 units per month, this can be regarded as an incremental progression towards your overarching goal of achieving 10,000 annual sales.

Then, envision the scenarios that will transpire should your objective be achieved. What will be the response of your team? How will you react?

This should provide sufficient assistance in formulating a strategic plan that will yield favorable outcomes. Ensure that your strategy incorporates the appropriate individuals. Which individual would be most suitable to assist you in addressing your objectives by overcoming the obstacles that may impede your progress?

Phase 3: Monitoring advancement

Given that the necessary actions have been initiated, it is now imperative to closely observe and assess their advancement. You are advised to diligently monitor the statistical data in order to evaluate its overall effectiveness.

You will be tasked with overseeing events that transpire throughout the course of the day, week, month, and beyond. It will demonstrate the extent to which you have made strides towards your objective. It will additionally ascertain the presence of any potential weaknesses.

Assume you are tracking persons in your sales department. The numerical analysis of an individual suggests the presence of apparent challenges. You are currently confronted with a predicament that necessitates prompt resolution.

Notify the individual that you have been closely monitoring their progress and it appears that they are currently encountering challenges. Determine the current state of affairs. Upon identifying the issue, formulate a comprehensive plan to facilitate their ongoing progress. If the issue appears to be pervasive, please engage in discussion with your team. Conduct a thorough examination of the issue and devise possible solutions. This is where your aptitude for problem-solving will be assessed.

Ensure personal and collective responsibility for addressing any difficulties that may arise. Use your time wisely. If it becomes necessary to make adjustments to the timelines, then let it be done.

As an individual in a position of leadership, it would be deemed imprudent to disregard the importance of monitoring progress. Particularly with regards to establishing and achieving financial objectives for your organization. In order to avoid being overshadowed, it is important to acknowledge that this can likewise have an impact on both your personal and your employees' long-term financial prospects.

Step 4: Attain and Strengthen

At this juncture, you have successfully implemented the requisite modifications to sustain your progress towards the attainment of your objectives. You and your team demonstrate efficient time management abilities, resulting in the expeditious achievement of the ambitious objectives you initially set. The objective has been successfully fulfilled, thus what is the subsequent course of action?

Repeat the process. One must recommence the process from the initial step and iterate it repeatedly. As a result of prior encounters, it significantly facilitates matters.

You are able to establish the objectives, compile a strategic plan, and monitor the progress accordingly. You are authorized to implement modifications whenever and wherever deemed appropriate. Additionally, you have the ability to identify and address concerns at an early stage, thereby averting their potential escalation into more significant challenges that may impede the efficiency and accomplishments of both yourself and your team.

Final Thoughts

As a leader, establishing and accomplishing objectives can be as uncomplicated as adhering to the 12-3-4 principle. This serves as your comprehensive guide to effectively aligning your and your team's objectives in the most astute and achievable manner possible. Produce a multitude of explicit and articulate statements.

Please be aware that it is necessary to monitor progress and establish a schedule for the completion of tasks. The more ambitious the objective, the greater the time required to achieve it (e.g., attaining 10000 sales within a year). It is necessary to undertake the process of decomposing that overarching objective into smaller, more manageable ones that can be achieved with greater expediency.

Ensure that you possess a comprehensive grasp of the precise objective, its measurable criteria, the appropriate methodology for its attainment, the importance it holds for your organization and its mission, and the scheduled completion date.

The Self-Disciplined Leader

Exercising self-discipline involves regulating one's temptations or desires in order to uphold the pursuit of a desired objective. The capacity to abstain from immediate satisfaction is pivotal to achieving success due to the crucial consequences that arise from this self-denial. A disciplined leader is destined for success as they possess the unwavering determination to persist, regardless of the allure of temptations.

It is imperative for leaders to possess self-discipline, as the absence of this quality will invariably have a negative impact on their subordinates, resulting in the inability to accomplish anything significant amidst such circumstances. Self-discipline is the key determinant of one's ability to maintain consistency in their actions. Self-discipline is the driving force that motivates individuals to rise from their comfortable bed at the early hour of 5 AM and embark upon their daily responsibilities. It is the driving force that prompts you to select the appropriate option, even when it is challenging.

The self-disciplined leader assumes the responsibility of ensuring the seamless functioning of operations and equitable allocation of tasks among all individuals involved. This leader exemplifies a profound comprehension of the principle that regardless of circumstances, the performance must proceed.

How to Become One:

The individual who exhibits unwavering self-discipline on a permanent basis is non-existent. Even the most resolute individuals in positions of leadership acknowledge that there are occasions when they find themselves on the verge of succumbing to temptation; nevertheless, by consistently opting for self-discipline on a daily basis, they find it more manageable to make the correct, albeit more challenging, choice." You can enhance your leadership abilities through the implementation of these strategies, ultimately cultivating self-discipline in the process.

Eliminate Distractions. Disruptions are ubiquitous in various environments, be it within professional or personal spheres. It is imperative for you to develop an understanding of these distractions and subsequently adopt measures to eradicate them. Similarly, it is important to demonstrate sensitivity towards the other members of the team by aiding their ability to identify elements that hinder their optimal performance. Moreover, offering constructive solutions to eliminate these obstacles would be beneficial.

As an example, if you and your team consistently engage in social media activity during designated project work hours, it is worth considering the potential benefits of implementing site restrictions during specific periods.

Take Scheduled Breaks. Frequently, there is an enhancement in efficiency when activities are executed with precision and regularity, as exemplified by daily productivity. Consider engaging in a task without a definitive timeline for completion; frequently, this will result in excessive exertion, leading to exhaustion and diminished motivation. It is not surprising that individuals who exert excessive effort often experience burnout.

In order to uphold self-discipline, it is imperative to recognize and comprehend both your own tempo as well as that of your team. It is essential to be conscious of the duration within which you are able to maintain productivity prior to experiencing the necessity of respite. For instance, the typical individual is capable of maintaining productive engagement in a task for a duration of two consecutive hours, after which a period of approximately 15 minutes of rest becomes necessary before proceeding to another two-hour interval. Establish a structured interval regimen for both yourself and your team, and observe the notable enhancement in overall performance.

Exert Positive Influence With Finesse

It is imperative for a leader to possess the ability to exert influence over their followers, and even extend their influence to other individuals. It is effortless to deliver a lecture or express one's thoughts, but it is often challenging to ensure a lasting impact and prevent the easy dissipation of one's message.

As a leader, it is crucial to recognize that the words you utter possess the potential to significantly influence individuals' lives, serving as a precipitating factor for transformative actions. However, how can one ascertain with certainty that they are exerting a positive influence and that such influence will endure? Peruse these recommendations to uncover the information.

Initially, acquaint yourself with your own identity. As previously stated, it is of utmost importance for individuals to possess self-awareness prior to assuming the role of a successful leader and impactful influencer. In the event that you find yourself befuddled regarding your identity and aspirations, one must not anticipate others to lend an ear or accord you respect. Familiarize yourself with your strengths and concurrently ascertain your weaknesses. By identifying your weaknesses, you can actively address and rectify them, thereby simultaneously safeguarding yourself. Do you find it effortless to captivate individuals through the use of your charming smile and engaging conversation? Make use of it. Do you possess the attributes to captivate individuals' interest through a professional demeanor in both appearance and communication? Good for you. Having knowledge of effective strategies to exert influence over others will significantly facilitate the process of persuading them to attentively consider your ideas or opinions.

It is important to bear in mind that consistent practice leads to flawless performance. It may sound trite, yet it holds true. As previously mentioned, conducting market tests will aid in determining the viability of producing specific products or services, as well as gauging customer reception towards them. Establish a definitive target demographic and devote focused efforts towards capturing their attention, at least for the time being. It is more efficient to conduct market tests with a select group of individuals, as opposed to attempting to reach a broad audience and obtaining inconclusive outcomes. Begin with modest investments, as eventually, the return on investment will significantly increase.

Learn how to Negotiate. Naturally, it is to be anticipated that not all individuals will immediately embrace your ideas and that favorable outcomes may not be instantaneously realized either. The essential factor for achieving success lies in mastering the art of effective communication, skillful negotiation, and, when warranted, the ability to reach mutually beneficial agreements. By adopting this approach, you can avail yourself of the opportunity to listen to the perspectives of others, instead of solely advancing your own ideas. Furthermore, by acquiring proficiency in the art of negotiation, one can assuredly secure advantageous transactions.

Individuals tend to grasp concepts more readily when they can contextualize them within real-life scenarios. This is due to their comprehension of the significant value of this product/service. In this manner, your sphere of influence can concurrently expand as individuals engage in discussions about your accomplishments and come to recognize its valuable impact on their own lives.

Establish well-defined objectives and cultivate a compelling long-term vision. Frequently, during the job application process, individuals are queried regarding their prospective aspirations. Certainly, your followers would undoubtedly be interested in acquainting themselves with your future aspirations as well. By adopting this approach, it will convey your unwavering confidence in your actions and reaffirm their affiliation with a reputable and secure organization. Your sphere of influence shall expand commensurately with the advancement of your objectives and the sharpening of your visionary outlook for the future.

Bridge the gap. Comprehend individuals' requirements and exclusions. Acquire a deeper understanding of the factors contributing to their inclination towards a particular product and the reasons for their potential disinterest in alternative options. It is imperative that individuals possess self-awareness and a comprehensive understanding of their surroundings, including the people and cultural context they are immersed in. By doing so, one can adeptly cater to the desires and expectations of others, thereby facilitating the creation of tailored solutions or products.

Determine the aspects in which you are excelling and identify the areas that require improvement. Do not attempt to rectify something that is functioning adequately; instead, focus your efforts on rectifying what requires improvement, paving the path to attaining success. Formulate effective strategies and arrange team-oriented activities or seminars to ensure a collective understanding of the tasks at hand, enabling collaborative efforts within the team.

Exemplify the qualities that would inspire others to willingly become your followers. How? Exhibit dedication and exemplify that despite your position as the superior, you shall not merely idly preside but actively engage in strenuous tasks. Exemplify a strong work ethic and collaborative mindset, both as a team contributor and not solely as a leader, to cultivate an expanding sphere of influence among your team members. Undoubtedly, the quality of the work environment would be significantly enhanced by implementing this approach.

Be logical. To persuade others of the value and practicality of your ideas, it is crucial for them to perceive your reasoning as both rational and logical. Demonstrate the coherence and rationality of your ideas. Ensure strategic planning while effectively articulating your concepts. Do not simply engage in verbal discussion, but rather construct a visually appealing PowerPoint presentation or a multimedia video to effectively convey your message." "Rather than solely engaging in verbal discourse, I suggest formulating a PowerPoint presentation or developing a video presentation as alternatives to articulate your point of view. To effectively capture the attention of others, it is imperative to ensure precise articulation of your intentions, exhibit a refined delivery devoid of any unprofessional tendencies, and accompany your proposal with an impassioned demeanor.

Be assertive. It is not deemed inappropriate to display assertiveness and engage in actions that capture people's attention. Why? In certain instances, it is imperative to capture individuals' attention through direct interaction rather than awaiting their receptiveness. You shall refrain from flaunting your knowledge or exerting effort to influence their comprehension directly, yet through your assertiveness, you will instill the perception that you possess valuable insights worthy of their attention. It is also permissible for you to scrutinize and question the ideas put forward by others, as this allows for a productive and constructive discourse regarding the necessary course of action. Do not hesitate to voice your thoughts.

And, it is crucial to consistently serve as a source of inspiration. Certainly, being a role model may present certain challenges. It possesses certain advantages, but it also harbors its drawbacks. If one lacks resilience, they may succumb to their shortcomings, resulting in feelings of inferiority. Bear in mind that these individuals, who are under your authority, regard you as a role model, regardless of their personal preferences. It is imperative that you possess the knowledge and understanding of how to demonstrate self-respect, as well as cultivate behaviors and interactions that command admiration and serve as a positive example to others. Conduct oneself with propriety, exhibit a commendable work demeanor, demonstrate equitable treatment towards others, while recognizing that one's actions will directly influence both personal reputation and professional image, thus emphasizing the importance of adhering to ethical practices. Motivate individuals not solely with your expressions but also through your behaviors. It is imperative to consistently emphasize to others that there are infinite possibilities and that collaboration facilitates the ease of tasks.

Staff Meetings

Staff meetings are essential for effective management. Regardless of whether you operate in the manufacturing sector or the service industry, convening staff meetings is imperative. In the absence of these meetings, the leadership would be bereft of crucial information regarding the ongoing progress of the company.

Recap and review.

Staff meetings provide a forum for employees to assess (i) the progress achieved thus far, and (ii) the tasks that still need to be addressed. A recap meeting may be arranged towards the end of the work week, specifically on Friday afternoon. This facilitates the opportunity for everyone to provide updates on the achievements made throughout the course of the week. A review meeting can promptly take place on Monday morning following the weekend, once the staff have reported for duty. This facilitates the readiness of the staff in anticipation of the upcoming week.

Schedule.

The regularity of staff meetings is contingent upon the nature of the enterprise. As an illustration, the majority of hospitals typically convene regular staff meetings at the onset of each day. The rationale behind this is that the provision of patient care, being an essential service, necessitates the possession of fully current patient status information by medical practitioners, nursing personnel, and emergency medical responders. Amidst the operations of a single enterprise, various departments may adhere to disparate timetables. As an illustration, the intensive care unit of a hospital necessitates bi-daily staff meetings, while the pediatric ward can suffice with two meetings per week.

Although staff meeting frequencies may vary, it is imperative for leaders to consider certain fundamental aspects when conducting these gatherings. Let us now examine several key ones.

End time.

Kindly inform the attendees about the scheduled conclusion time of the meeting. This instills a sense of calm and reassurance among all individuals involved, as they are aware that they can proceed with their daily activities, whether that be returning to their workstation or departing for their residence. A considerable number of managers possess the practice of commencing the meeting punctually, ensuring that the meeting endures until all attendees have had the opportunity to express their thoughts. While this approach may demonstrate consideration towards the staff, it typically proves ineffective as individuals often have a proclivity to continue speaking unabated once provided with the microphone, requiring explicit instruction to cease. The aforementioned observation applies to numerous managers who preside over the meeting, engaging in lengthy discourse as a manifestation of their inflated sense of significance.

Meetings of excessive length eventually become purposeless, as the attention and focus of the participants diminish, leading to a loss of comprehension of the discussions at hand. Therefore, it is advisable for a proficient manager to formally communicate that the duration of the day's meeting will be strictly limited to a specified time, without any extensions. As the moderator of the meeting, a competent manager bears the duty of time management, which entails interrupting speakers in order to facilitate equitable participation and ensure the progress of the meeting.

Purpose.

At the onset of the meeting, it is customary for a managerial figure to declare the objective of the gathering. It could constitute a comprehensive assessment meeting to evaluate forthcoming developments; alternatively, it may serve a distinct purpose, such as presenting a status update on a specific program or project.

A critical duty that an effective manager must fulfill in relation to a general or specific meeting entails ensuring that discussions stay on track. Specifically, if a staff member introduces a particular matter during a general meeting, it is imperative for the manager to kindly request that the individual save their comments for a subsequent meeting solely dedicated to that issue. Conversely, should a staff member start addressing general topics during a meeting that was convened to specifically address a certain matter, the manager should interject and politely instruct the person to raise those concerns at the next general meeting.

In a similar vein, a proficient manager might communicate a policy wherein individuals are encouraged to share their insights or ideas for the collective advantage of the entire group. However, if an individual merely intends to provide an update on their individual work, it is deemed unnecessary to impose upon the time of others who may not be genuinely interested in their progress.

Many individuals at meetings tend to engage in unnecessary speech due to the underlying motivation of asserting their presence. This behavior stems from a concern that remaining silent may lead the supervisor to assume they lack tasks or responsibilities. Hence, it is imperative for a proficient manager to assure the staff members that only individuals with meaningful contributions towards the collective welfare of the group are encouraged to voice their opinions, while others are expected to maintain silence.

Keep it short.

One factor contributing to the tedious nature of staff meetings is the inadequate ability of the staff speakers to concisely deliver their comments or questions. It is incumbent upon the competent manager to guarantee that. Among the five interrogative prompts encompassing "Who?" "What?" "When?" "Where?" and "How?", it is the inquiry beginning with "How?" which tends to elicit a lengthy and elaborate response. Therefore, it is imperative for a proficient manager to request the team members who present a "How?" inquiry to arrange a subsequent meeting for a comprehensive response to the query.

Enable all individuals to express their opinions.

A staff meeting provides a platform for all participants to express themselves, whether in the form of providing updates, addressing issues, or sharing concerns. Therefore, permit each individual the opportunity to express their thoughts. After the member has addressed the matter, it is now within your authority to determine whether the raised issue should be deliberated upon during the current session or postponed to a subsequent meeting. Granting employees the authorization to express themselves fosters a sense of recognition and appreciation, affirming their status as integral team contributors and signaling that their perspectives and ideas hold significance.

Bottlenecks and progress.

Typically, staff meetings serve the purpose of achieving two objectives. An option available is to provide updates on impediments encountered during the execution of allocated responsibilities. The factors contributing to these hindrances may vary, ranging from insufficient expertise to execute the task, to inadequate resources for its implementation. It would be advisable for managers to promptly identify and acknowledge any barriers encountered, and subsequently convene a post-meeting session to effectively resolve the identified issue or issues. Should the manager choose to procrastinate in addressing these bottlenecks, there may be significant repercussions. An exemplification in this case would be the imposition of substantial demurrage fees in response to the delay in customs clearance at various port and airport checkpoints.

Progress reports, undoubtedly, bring great satisfaction to a manager's ears.

Staff Management Qualities

It is imperative for all leaders to not solely prioritize enhancing their communication skills, but also to diligently cultivate their competence in team management. A leader effectively oversees a significant multitude of individuals. In spite of the exceptional communicative skills possessed by certain leaders, there exist additional aspects that require their proficient attention. They are required to demonstrate outstanding management qualities in order to effectively oversee the staff and optimize the potential of each individual team member.

First characteristic: Proficiency in Task Delegation

Developing a refined brand vision is crucial in order to cultivate a cohesive and skilled team. Ensure that you possess the willingness to place trust in your employees in regards to executing the assigned tasks and ensuring their alignment with your overarching vision. This measure will effectively ensure that you do not remain trapped at your current proficiency level. In order to progress to the subsequent stages of your project, it is imperative that you place your trust in the capabilities of your staff.

As a leader, it is imperative that you develop confidence in the competence of your staff to successfully complete any assigned task. It is imperative that you possess an understanding of the strengths and weaknesses of all individuals in order to effectively assign tasks to the suitable departments. Mastering and conscientiously attending to the art of task delegation is an indispensable capability that demands your attention as your enterprise progresses. If you fail to place trust in your team and instead take on tasks independently, there will be a cumulative buildup of work. As you overexert yourself in an attempt to manage the workload, the quality of your output will progressively diminish, resulting in financial losses.

One must evaluate and recognize the individual strengths of each team member in order to effectively delegate tasks. Discover the individual preferences and areas of expertise of your personnel, subsequently leveraging those strengths to maximize productivity. If individuals have a genuine passion for the task they have been assigned, it is probable that they will exhibit enhanced effort and carry out the task with reduced difficulty.

Engaging in such actions can undoubtedly benefit both you and your team member, as it will serve to demonstrate your confidence in them and their abilities.

The sense of trust instilled by your superior is highly valued and cherished by the majority of employees, who would be reluctant to compromise it in any way. They will consistently invest greater effort into their endeavors and derive heightened satisfaction from their work pursuits. Additionally, it allows you to allocate greater time and effort towards more complex and demanding tasks. This straightforward equilibrium holds the potential to greatly enhance the productivity of your business.

Second Criterion – Capacity to Evoke Inspiration

The process of launching a business frequently entails meticulous assessment, particularly when embarking on a nascent endeavor. It is imperative that you evoke inspiration within your team to envision the same future that you perceive. In simple terms, it is imperative that each and every one of you maintain a unified focus. As an exemplary leader, it is inappropriate to impose upon others the obligation to adhere to your principles or to expect their unwavering allegiance. Rather than imposing the expectation for your staff to replicate your level of energy and enthusiasm, endeavor to engage them in your undertakings. It is imperative that you demonstrate to them the extent of your desire to achieve your team's objective.

If you assemble individuals who share your circumstances, it is probable that you would attain your objective with greater ease. Nevertheless, there are instances in which your mindset may not align with that of your team, and in such circumstances, there is no need to replace individuals in order to achieve favorable outcomes. It is necessary to provide them with inspiration and enlighten them about the reasons underlying your actions. This presents a more favorable approach to foster their motivation towards collectively realizing your shared vision.

Criterion 3 – Benevolence

It is imperative for every leader to possess the knowledge and skill of properly acknowledging and rewarding the exceptional contributions of their team members. Implementing a incentivization framework within your enterprise serves as an effective means to communicate to your employees that their productivity and diligent efforts shall yield satisfactory remuneration. Equitable compensation for commensurate labor, indeed. None of the leaders around the globe have ever achieved success in solitude. They have a team. They collaborate with colleagues and demonstrate their commitment to maintaining cohesiveness within the team. The most effective manner of ensuring the well-being of your team is by demonstrating your appreciation for their efforts through acts of generosity.

In order to effectively lead your team, it is imperative to actively listen to their input and acknowledge their dedication and positive contributions to a project through the provision of incentives and rewards. The rewards need not be extravagant. Modest offerings or modest expressions of gratitude are sufficient to instill a spirit of excellence within them and will serve as a catalyst for their unwavering dedication.

The objective of the leader is to demonstrate

Peter instructs us to serve as role models to the congregation (1 Peter 5:3). In Christian leadership, emphasis is placed on demonstrating rather than verbalizing. One guides individuals by demonstrating the path instead of merely instructing them about it. A primary impetus behind assuming a leadership role should be to serve as an exemplar for others. You exemplify the transformative power of God in the lives of individuals, thereby encouraging others to emulate your example.

Paul declares, "Emulate my example as I emulate the example of Christ" (1 Corinthians 11:1). What a powerful challenge. May I express the equivalent sentiment to those who are following me? Do I ever advocate for actions that I myself do not follow? Instructing others on proper behavior is considerably simpler compared to actively exemplifying the expected conduct. However, when instructing your subordinates to engage in prayer, it is imperative that you also exemplify a penchant for prayer. It is imperative that you arrive early when instructing them to attend the meeting punctually. This standard poses a significant challenge for the majority of leaders. Pose the following question to yourself: "In the event that all individuals within my organization possessed similar attributes as me, how would this impact its overall character?"

Leaders have the propensity to effortlessly transform into dictators who issue instructions to others while failing to provide a role model themselves. Jesus vehemently admonished the Pharisees for precisely this type of leadership. The Pharisees, through their actions, assumed a position of authority and dominion over those beneath them. According to Peter, one should refrain from exerting dominance over individuals under their care. The phrase "lording it over" signifies the misuse of authority, the act of leveraging one's position to enforce compliance, or the exploitation of power for personal gain.

The act of lording can be observed when we:

• Decline to engage in challenges

• Verbally abuse people

• Request reparation or entitlements

• Manipulate others

Coercion is not employed in Christian leadership. Individuals have the liberty to choose whether or not to adhere. Your sole ability lies in drawing individuals towards you by means of authentic modesty and selflessness. Influence is acquired by demonstrating yourself as an exemplar, thereby eliciting a desire in others to emulate you.

As a leader, you have the power to either enhance your own standing or uplift those around you. According to the scripture in 2 Corinthians 13:10, Paul expresses his desire to exercise his authority in a gentle manner upon his arrival, as the authority bestowed upon him by the Lord has the purpose of nurturing and edifying rather than causing harm. It is evident that individuals require competent and steadfast leadership. I am not suggesting that you stop exercising good leadership, but that you must exercise it from a position of love and for the benefit of people, not yourself.

If your intention is to exemplify leadership, it is imperative that you meticulously scrutinize your own lifestyle to guarantee that you are a meritorious role model. In certain contexts, one may exert dominance in areas where personal fidelity has not been demonstrated; however, true leadership can solely be achieved by directing individuals along a course that has already been experienced. Are others able to emulate your behavior as a model?

The primary objective of the leader is to ensure fulfillment.

Peter's ultimate objective for all Christian leaders is to gratify the "Supreme Shepherd." Peter serves as a reminder in this passage that we have been entrusted with the responsibility of shepherding God's flock. God holds the esteemed title of the "Supreme Shepherd" (1 Peter 5:4), occupying the apex of the organizational hierarchy. The congregation belongs to him, not to me. In order to excel in leadership, it is imperative to acknowledge and respect both divine and human authority. You are employed by Him, serving under His authority as well as the authority of others. Referring to Him as "Lord" signifies that He possesses the authority to govern all aspects of your existence. On numerous occasions, spiritual leaders may inadvertently overlook the fact that God's presence is not physically tangible within their immediate vicinity, causing them to lose sight of the accountability they hold towards God. As a consequence, they may exhibit behaviors more aligned with dictatorial tendencies rather than embodying the nurturing role of a shepherd. However, your intention should be to fulfill the expectations of your superior.

Rather than aspiring to fulfill the wishes of the Lord, one might frequently be inclined to aspire to fulfill the desires of others. Your physical being yearns for acceptance, desiring recognition and praise. Peter emphasizes the importance of engaging in labor not to seek validation from others, but rather to seek validation from one's divine Master.

Peter also advocates for your consideration of future prospects. He speaks of the moment when the "Supreme Shepherd manifests." At present, He might remain concealed from your perception and on occasion, you may inadvertently overlook His vigilant observation of your endeavors. Nonetheless, rest assured that He shall materialize in due course. Does that pledge evoke a sense of excitement within you? Have you been the type of leader who will take pleasure in witnessing the arrival of the Master? On that day, there will be individuals who will lower their heads in a gesture of contrition. Witness shall befall upon them as their works succumb to the consuming flames. However, individuals who have dutifully fulfilled their roles as leaders will be bestowed with an esteemed symbol of honor known as the 'crown of glory' (according to 1 Peter 5:4).

I am filled with anticipation and joyous anticipation when contemplating the day when Jesus will arrive and bestow upon me a regal adornment. Each adherent will be granted a recompense, however, Peter specifically addresses devoted leaders, those who have dedicated themselves to the service of the Lord.

This reward is definite. Peter does not express the belief that one might receive their rewards, but rather asserts that they will. While leaders of the world may reap their benefits in this earthly realm, it is in the heavenly realm where you shall receive yours. Although there are certainly benefits and rewards for those who display strong leadership in this life, the ultimate and everlasting rewards reside in the realm of heaven. That crown will endure eternally.

Envision the celestial realm where, in a sequential manner, God summons Christian leaders individually to receive their well-deserved recompense. What will be His assessment of your leadership abilities? I aspire to listen to the phrase, "Behold, a leader who responded to My summons and guided with My benevolence."

This enduring viewpoint ensures the integrity of our intentions. It directs our attention towards devoutly serving Christ, maintaining a heart untainted by impurities. Allocate a sufficient amount of time for introspection and thoroughly evaluate your underlying motivations. What is the reason for your role as a leader? Take a moment to ponder the reasons that Peter presents in this passage and permit the divine presence to communicate with your innermost being.

Recognize The Importance Of Your Millennial Workforce And Afford Them Opportunities For Development

As previously mentioned, Millennials possess a fondness for embracing challenges and aspire to enhance their proficiency in their respective endeavors. In the event that individuals perceive a lack of growth in their professional pursuits and a dearth of challenges, their engagement with the task diminishes and they swiftly become disinterested and bored. When confronted with ennui, they commence actively seeking alternative prospects and subsequently depart from your establishment.

Based on the analysis provided by Ketti Salemme, a seasoned communication manager employed at TINYpulse, it can be observed that individuals belonging to the Millennial generation exhibit a tendency to disregard established norms related to workplace dynamics and professional growth. They are actively pursuing accelerated expansion and advancement, displaying impatience towards the attainment of a promotion.

In order to retain your millennial workforce within your organization and leverage their talents and knowledge, it is imperative to provide them with opportunities for growth and development. Therefore, in order to foster a sense of inclusion and fully leverage the Millennials' talents within your organization, it is imperative that you demonstrate the utmost appreciation for them and afford them the chance to flourish and advance.

Allow me to present to you a method by which you may accomplish the task.

Provide them with stimulating and demanding assignments

Assign complex and engaging projects to your generation Y employees in order to sustain their enthusiasm for work and their loyalty towards your organization. Facilitate their engagement in assignments and undertakings that promote rapid experiential growth and acquisition of knowledge. This initiative will aid in the preservation of your existing Millennial workforce while fostering the development of skillsets among promising new hires.

Familiarize yourself with the strengths of your millennial employees and utilize them appropriately.

According to a recent study conducted by Gallup, it was found that employees belonging to Generation Y possess an understanding of their strengths and desire the organization they are employed with to acknowledge and appreciate both their capabilities and their valuable contributions to the company.

Should your millennial employees exhibit discontent and dissatisfaction, it is plausible that their discontentment stems from a lack of recognition for their competence and skills, resulting in their placement in departments that fail to optimize their capabilities to the fullest extent. Consequently, they are likely to face limited prospects for substantial progress as millennials tend to withhold their full commitment and strive for excellence only in activities they find enjoyable or possess competence in.

In order to foster the development and advancement of your organization, it is imperative to conduct a comprehensive analysis of the Millennials under your employ and discern their areas of expertise. Once you have determined their areas of expertise, assign them to suitable departments and positions that allow for the optimal utilization of their skills and support the realization of their distinctive capabilities.

For example, in the event that you have assigned a Millennial who holds an accounting degree to the accounting department, it would be advisable to inquire whether this employee possesses genuine interest in the field of accounting. Should the employee express dissatisfaction with accounting, it is recommended to reassign them to a department that aligns more fittingly with their skills and interests. Likewise, in the event that a Generation Y employee finds gratification in outdoor activities, but currently occupies the role of your personal secretary, it is advisable to provide the employee with a more stimulating and exhilarating task.

In order to ascertain the strengths and preferred activities of your millennial employees, it will be necessary for you to establish a connection with them. This will facilitate a more comprehensive comprehension of their distinctive qualities, talents, and attributes, enabling you to employ them effectively and appropriately. When millennials are given the opportunity to engage in tasks aligned with their skillsets and passions, they naturally exhibit a strong commitment to their work, fostering both individual and organizational growth.

Offer Rapid Promotions

Promoting your millennial employees rapidly and at an accelerated pace is another effective approach to facilitate their growth and sustain their engagement within your organization. Rather than granting them promotions following 3, 5, or 10 years, it would be advisable to consider promoting them on a semi-annual or annual basis. This strategy ensures that your millennials are provided with a reward following each incremental period, thereby maintaining their satisfaction.

Given the limitation of not being able to promote an employee to the same managerial level within a six-month timeframe, it is advisable to generate a multitude of fresh positions and augment the duties and responsibilities of each role. As an example, one could consider the fragmentation of the role of a Marketing Manager into four or five distinct positions. With each level, the addition of new responsibilities and a commensurate increment in remuneration would be implemented.

Ensure that their job is in accordance with their interests and values

An alternative approach, that can prove successful in facilitating the growth and engagement of your millennial workforce, is to harmonize their activities with their fundamental values and principles. Determine the core values and aspirations of your millennial employees as individuals, and subsequently seek to integrate those aspects into their respective roles and responsibilities. This adds an element of heightened excitement and heightened challenge to their work, thereby instilling a strong sense of genuine value for each individual millennial.

For example, in the case of a millennial employee who exhibits a proclivity for socializing and holds a position within the Human Resources department, it could be advantageous to designate said individual as the leader of a survey pertaining to matters of personnel management. In this manner, you foster the integration of their personal interests with their professional responsibilities, thereby ensuring their active engagement in their work. Identify the concerns and values of the Millennial generation and integrate them with their professional responsibilities.

Please take this advice into consideration. Should you choose to take such action, your millennial workforce and subordinates will derive great satisfaction from their professional endeavors, as you will be actively fostering their swift advancement and consistently providing them with motivation and support.

Be a Visionary

If you lack a clear vision for the individuals under your guidance, your progress on the hierarchy of leadership will be severely limited. Each successful leader possesses the quality of foresight. The notion that vision plays a crucial role in distinguishing exceptional leaders from their counterparts is widely accepted.

The vision should serve as the foundation for establishing your goals. The vision encompasses the comprehensive outcome you aspire to witness, serving as the underlying rationale behind your objectives. The vision serves as the primary rationale behind your objectives. With a clear vision, your objectives and aspirations acquire greater clarity and tangibility. Vision functions as an intrinsic driving force that continuously propels one's trajectory. A well-defined vision serves as a compelling source of inspiration for the individuals under your guidance. It inspires passion. A leader devoid of a vision is merely an elevated member of the team: true leadership encompasses much more than that.

Leadership Tip #13 Embrace a forward-thinking mindset. Acquire comprehensive knowledge about your organization (or the entity you aspire to be insightful about). Consequently, undertake an examination of comparable entities and their operational practices. Subsequently, proceed to contemplate strategies that can enhance the efficiency, productivity, and creativity of your organization. It entails an examination of a company's future prospects and the conceptualization of strategies to forge a transformative and more promising trajectory.

Consistently refer to the vision as "the" vision rather than "my" vision. It is imperative for the team to comprehend that all members are collectively striving towards a larger objective that surpasses the significance of any single individual. When individuals perceive the discussion to revolve around "your" vision, it has the potential to instill feelings of exclusion from the overarching objectives and reinforce the notion that they are solely contributing to your personal gain, ultimately diminishing their level of productivity.

Having a clear vision, deep passion, well-defined goals, strategic plans, and taking decisive action all contribute to achieving great things!

Never Stop Learning

To garner admiration and deference from subordinates, it is imperative to acquire profound expertise in one's role.

Remain informed of all ongoing advancements within the organization. Acquire novel tools that can serve as positive catalysts for enhancing the lives of those under your guidance. Once an individual believes they have attained complete knowledge of their company or leadership skills, their credibility as a leader begins to diminish.

Leadership Principle #14 Possess comprehensive knowledge in your field. Acquire comprehensive knowledge pertaining to your role, thoroughly familiarize yourself with the intricacies of your job; Your range of knowledge should not be confined solely to your area of expertise, but should encompass strategies for improving leadership abilities as well. The more effective your leadership, the more well-developed your employees will be. Employees who have undergone significant professional growth and development are inclined to exhibit enhanced efficiency and consistently produce superior quality work.

Engage in literature, partake in educational conferences, subscribe to reputable leadership platforms and blogs, listen to audio resources, and emulate the guidance of a mentor. Continuous learning is of utmost importance, specifically in terms of enhancing leadership skills, as this knowledge proves invaluable across various domains.

Once you develop and nurture these essential leadership attributes, you are on a promising path towards becoming an exceptional leader.

Taking that into consideration, we will explore strategies for exerting a constructive impact on the lives of individuals under your supervision, enabling them to cultivate self-assurance and acquire the necessary skills to potentially assume leadership positions in the future, should they aspire to do so.

Please Ensure The Stimulation Of One's Intellect

As a leader, it is imperative to foster an environment where not only your personal learning and growth are prioritized, but also where your subordinates are equipped with the knowledge and skills to maximize their potential and effectively navigate their circumstances. Intellectual stimulation is fostered when leaders inspire their subordinates to exhibit creativity and ingenuity. As a leader, it is imperative to instill in your followers the belief that they possess an inherent potential for greatness, and that through diligent efforts, intellectual acumen, and unwavering passion in their pursuits, remarkable achievements can be attained.

"How to cultivate creativity and enhance intellectual stimulation:

Presented herein are several straightforward techniques to ensure that one's followers are afforded ample opportunities for creativity, thereby precluding any sense of stagnation. The most undesirable outcome would be a lack of development and progress among your personnel as well as within the organization as a whole.

Offer challenges. Facilitate circumstances that empower your followers to demonstrate their abilities and assert themselves. This can be achieved through the implementation of training programs, educational seminars, and collaborative team building initiatives. In this manner, it becomes possible to engage in playing games while also facilitating collaborative ideation sessions.

Ask questions. At times, a chief shortcoming exhibited by certain leaders is their failure to solicit inquiries from their subordinates. They possess an unwarranted belief in their omniscience, subsequently resulting in a static state. Even if you perceive yourself as highly intelligent, it is important to remember that there is no harm in seeking clarifications and seeking assistance from others. A competent leader possesses the ability to attentively consider and incorporate the input and recommendations of others.

Cultivating a mindset that embraces self-assurance and capability. Do you recall the statement made by former US President Obama? If they assert that the proposed task is unattainable, our resolute response is to affirm its possibility. It is imperative that you instill within your personnel the unwavering belief that regardless of external skepticism, their internal conviction in their ability to accomplish remarkable feats is paramount, particularly when accompanied by diligent effort. Maintain a constructive demeanor within the professional environment, and undoubtedly the circumstances will improve for everyone involved.

Don't stick to norms. Do not hesitate to venture into uncharted territories and transcend your self-imposed constraints. Engage in innovative and unconventional thinking. If an individual presents an excellent concept which aligns with the values and objectives of your organization, seize the opportunity to pursue it. If an individual puts forth a novel proposition that you have yet to experience, embrace it. It is imperative to possess the knowledge and skills to navigate the unpredictable nature of change. By adopting this approach, you can be assured that regardless of the passage of time or any unforeseen circumstances, your success is guaranteed. You will not make a significant impact if you confine yourself to your past accomplishments. Do not hesitate to embrace opportunities for risks.

Establish an environment conducive to fostering creativity within the workplace. Permit your followers to display items of their choosing on their desks, on the condition that said items do not possess derogatory characteristics. Permit them to adorn their desks with collages, their preferred quotes, or any personal item of their choosing. A vibrant and whimsical work environment is consistently more preferable than a monotonous and drab one. By adopting this approach, one can foster increased enthusiasm among their employees, who will come to perceive them not only as a superior, but also as a trusted acquaintance.

Observe. Gain the ability to carefully perceive and analyze the happenings in the external environment, enabling yourself to derive inspiration for potential actions and determine the appropriate course for personal development. Acquire the ability to recognize the inevitability of change and comprehend that in order for individuals to connect with you and engage with what you provide, they must be assured of its usefulness to them, as well as your understanding of their desires and necessities.

Don't overwork. Depart from the office premises upon the conclusion of the designated work hours, allocate an appropriate duration for restful repose, and subsequently observe that on the subsequent day, one shall ascertain their preparedness and genuine enthusiasm to engage in work once more. Do not permit excessive workload for your followers or yourself, as it would impede optimal cognitive functioning. A mind that possesses the ability to rest is indicative of a creative nature.

Use Mood Boards. Mood Boards can be comprised of corkboards, allowing individuals to freely pin diverse elements such as their aspirations, desired travel destinations, or current emotional reflections. Furthermore, an alternative option is available through the utilization of the website Pinterest, which may potentially be more convenient for your particular needs. Ultimately, if one is able to mentally conceive of a possibility, it becomes feasible as they are inclined to devote greater effort and enthusiasm towards its realization.

Furthermore, it is imperative to acknowledge the significance of acquiring new knowledge on a daily basis. Continuously engage in the pursuit of reading books, perusing captivating articles, and familiarizing yourself with diverse individuals. By doing so, you will significantly augment your understanding of the world in which you reside.

By bearing these suggestions in mind, one can assuredly achieve intellectual stimulation.

Simplifying Your Thought Processes and Ceasing Excessive Rumination

Were you aware that your mind has the potential to become cluttered? Similar to the presence of disarray in a household, a multitude of disorderly thoughts can occupy one's mind. Although a certain level of clutter is expected, an excessive quantity thereof can result in a restless state of mind. It possesses the potential to disrupt cognitive processes, impair one's capacity to achieve restful sleep, and influence emotional states. When one's mind is in a state of disarray, it signifies an endeavor to move in numerous directions concurrently. Due to the absence of a definitive trajectory, your mental state lingers in a state of uncertainty. Your cognitive faculties exhibit a state of neutrality, hindering their effective navigation through the various tasks encountered during the course of your day.

The presence of such excessive disarray can induce feelings of irritability and anxiety. Both of those states are detrimental to both your mental well-being and your interpersonal relationships. One might encounter oneself trapped in a state of reminiscence, anxiously contemplating one's prospects, or generally perceiving a pessimistic outlook on one's existence. Your thoughts might be consistently preoccupied with a list of tasks that remains perpetually incomplete. Anger can be the outward expression of these various emotions and mental chaos. The mind and body necessitate a mechanism through which to organize and cope with the clutter within one's thoughts. Frequently, it is through the manifestation of intense emotional outbursts.

Decluttering Tips 101

Managing cognitive overload is analogous to managing physical clutter within the confines of your residence. It is imperative that you commence by structuring your thoughts and establishing a designated space for them.

Address each item individually. It is considerably more manageable to address a problem through incremental progress, as opposed to attempting to resolve it comprehensively with a single overarching solution.

Presented herein are several strategies that can be employed to organize and clear one's thoughts.

Please articulate your thoughts on paper.

The cognitive prowess of your brain is truly remarkable, yet when inundated with numerous lines of thinking, it becomes ensnared in confusion. However, there is no need for you to retain all of those thoughts within your cognitive faculties. Instead, write them down. Transcribing your thoughts onto paper alleviates mental strain and facilitates revisiting each idea at a later time. If they represent a list of tasks to be completed, it is possible to display them on the refrigerator. If these are your profound contemplations and sentiments, it is recommended that you preserve them within a personal diary, intended solely for your perusal.

Move On:

Prolonged fixation on past events can have detrimental effects on one's well-being. The choices and actions that you might have desired to make, or approached in a different manner, instances where opportunities were not seized, the end of relationships, moments of humiliation, and so forth, the enumeration persists. One is unable to alter the course of history, but can solely acquire wisdom from it. Every individual is prone to errors, therefore it is important to grant yourself forgiveness and refrain from engaging in self-criticism. If you persist in harboring past grievances, endeavor to extend forgiveness towards the other party for their transgressions. Have enough self-respect to release it, and proceed forward.

Learn to Prioritize:

If your thoughts are preoccupied with your various obligations, establish a concise inventory of tasks that require immediate attention. Contrary to the disorganized state of your mind, it is important to recognize that not everything carries the same level of urgency or importance. After compiling your list, focus on prioritizing and executing those tasks as a primary objective. Once you have accomplished all of those items on the list, proceed to the less critical tasks. In addition to experiencing a sense of accomplishment, you will also notice a gradual alleviation of the burden associated with your tasks.

Create an Auto-Pilot Habit:

Select minor undertakings in your daily routine that you will consistently execute in a standardized manner. For instance, establish a structured nightly regimen. Stroll through the premises and engage in a brief 10-minute organization session. Ensure that the dishes have been washed, blankets have been tidied, lights have been extinguished, and the bathroom is well-maintained. Prepare your morning coffee and schedule the brew using a timer. Subsequently, indulge in a soothing shower or bath, don fresh sleepwear, and recline to rest for the evening. Developing a nightly ritual that involves finalizing the events of the day and making preparations for the following day can contribute to a sense of fulfillment. On the subsequent day, you arise with a sense of preparedness to commence a fresh day. After you have successfully established this consistent pattern, it will gradually transform into an ingrained practice, effortlessly executed without conscious effort.

Clean:

Be it from your place of residence, professional establishment, automobile, or any combination thereof. Disorderliness in your tangible surroundings leads to mental disorder. Dedicate sufficient time to establish a pristine environment that will extend to your psychological well-being.

Meditate or Do Yoga:

Engaging in these activities imparts cognitive skills to help attain a state of tranquility. Your objective is to center your attention on the present moment, engage in deliberate deep breaths, and allocate sufficient periods of rest for your body. Participating in endeavors that offer moments of respite allows your mind to obtain a period of rest. This brief intermission allows your mind to cease dwelling on the most dire outcome, not to mention that the respite can gradually unclutter and begin to rationalize all the thoughts occupying your mind. If one allows oneself regular moments of pause, one will observe that a state of tranquility permeates various facets of both one's day and life. You shall henceforth alleviate any potential frustration stemming from encountering poor drivers, enduring lengthy queues, or succumbing to agitation when circumstances deviate from your desired outcomes.

The Phenomenon Of Love

Love remains a perpetual preoccupation and an eternal focal point in the hearts and minds of all individuals. Certainly, the underlying driving force behind human interactions frequently revolves around the longing for the sensation of affection in various manifestations. The significance of love holds substantial ramifications for leadership. Specifically, the extent to which leaders recognize the significance of affection in their personal lives and in the lives of others can be the determining factor in the accomplishment or downfall of their endeavors.

Contrary to being inconsequential or unfeasible, the desire to convey affection is essential for proficient leadership. This is the case since, ultimately, a leader's drive is conveyed to others through numerous nuanced means. Leaders whose actions are deemed to prioritize their own personal interests frequently engender discord, animosity, and a lack of allegiance. Alternatively, individuals who anchor their actions in sincere empathy and genuine concern for others can foster the allegiance and backing necessary to achieve even the most challenging objectives.

Love Versus Lust

In reality, despite its pervasive presence in the minds of individuals, love is frequently misconstrued. Love encompasses a depth beyond the mere experience of agreeable emotions or the gratification derived from physical encounters. Often, what individuals commonly refer to as love can be equated to sentimentality or the pursuit of purely sensual gratifications. This implies that for numerous individuals, what is often perceived as love may in fact be merely a manifestation of egocentric tendencies or carnal desires.

While individuals are persistently influenced by the conflicting forces of affection and self-indulgent desire, they possess the autonomy to discern and make a conscious decision between these two dynamics. The outcome of every leadership endeavor hinges exclusively on the extent to which a leader embraces the force of selfless affection.

This does not inevitably imply a seamless and effortless progression of events. Actions that demonstrate mature love are executed with a demeanor of sincerity and comprehension. While it is true that the truth has the potential to cause discomfort, there are instances where the pursuit of a greater good may necessitate leaders to confront inconvenient truths and take resolute action. Truly, love remains bereft of significance unless it rests upon a foundation of truthfulness. Leaders must possess a profound understanding, expertise, and astuteness to effectively demonstrate their affection in accordance with the given circumstances.

Hence, notwithstanding its occasional tenderness, love can also exhibit severity. Occasionally, a leader might require individuals to make arduous sacrifices for the sake of their own welfare. Regardless of the scenario, be it one where actions come across as kind or cruel, the crucial aspect always lies in the underlying motivation. A leader who exhibits selflessness conducts themselves in a manner akin to a devoted mother, occasionally employing disciplinary measures with the goal of facilitating the proper growth and development of those under their care. Leaders must consciously opt to uphold a state of awareness that prioritizes the well-being of others, irrespective of outward facades.

It is important for leaders to bear in mind, as part of their routine contemplation, that throughout history, the downfall of remarkable individuals and the collapse of mighty empires have often been attributed to the overwhelming influence of desire and the lack of mastery over their physical desires. Their excessive focus on their own needs and desires led them to give in to the allure of using people for personal gain, instead of prioritizing their welfare. However, it is imperative for contemporary leaders to keep in mind that leadership fundamentally entails the embodiment of altruistic affection.

The Ethereal Essence of the Human Species.

A method of cultivating a mature affection is by perceiving each individual as a divine entity, cherished by the Almighty and under His vigilant supervision. Undoubtedly, there resides a divine essence within the core of every sentient being, and it is attainable to transcend towards self-actualization, thus discovering and embracing this facet of divinity both within oneself and in fellow human beings. Even in the absence of such a depth of comprehension, if one were to bear in mind that there exists a divine element within every individual and that this divinity bestows personal concern for every human being, it would be possible to express reverence and esteem towards all.

The human species possesses an inherent spiritual or divine essence akin to that of God Himself, albeit with finite capabilities unlike God's infinite ones. Put simply, individuals possess the same essential qualities as God, albeit in varying degrees. The spiritual component in question constitutes the soul, referred to as the atma or higher self, which encompasses the everlasting essence wherein the divine aspect resides within every individual. Engaging in thoughts, expressions, or deeds that are specifically aimed at an individual's elevated state of being will yield significantly more advantageous and enduring outcomes compared to those that lack such intent.

In fact, every individual is comprised of three constituents, namely the physical body (which encompasses the subtle or etheric body), the astral body, and the soul, which represents the elevated self, the guiding essence resembling that of a deity. Throughout the annals of history, civilizations have harbored the knowledge that humanity possesses an elevated essence, such that even in the face of mortal demise, merely a cessation of the corporeal vessel, the spirit endures. As an illustration, in the context of ancient Greece, Socrates, prior to his execution, expressed the belief that while his physical body may perish, his immortal soul would endure. Individuals who possess an appreciation for these various dimensions of human experience will refrain from confining themselves solely to materialistic or psychological comprehension. Instead, they will recognize the paramount significance of the spiritual realm, to which the soul is inherently connected.

One cannot extend love to others if sufficient self-love is absent, for it is inherently improbable to offer or impart what one does not already possess within oneself. Frequently, leadership poses challenges due to issues surrounding individual personalities or strong affiliations with concepts such as nationalism, racism, sexism, or tribalism. In order to effectively address such matters, it is imperative to cultivate an unwavering affection that originates from self-love, recognizing the inherent divine essence within oneself. The adoration for oneself does not encompass admiration for the physical or intellectual aspects, but rather shows reverence for the essence of one's being. There is no requirement for you to devote attention to the comfort of the body, the stimulation of the senses, or the pursuit of adulation or financial gain from others. Furthermore, it can be acknowledged that the physical form, sensory faculties, and mental faculties merely serve as transient disguises assumed by the spirit.

Activities imbued with love are in alignment with the cosmic order. Individuals who exhibit disharmony with the universe tend to attract negativity towards their existence, while those who demonstrate harmony engage in constructive and productive actions, thereby safeguarding themselves against any detrimental consequences.

Love as a Safeguarding Power

As a leader, throughout the execution of your responsibilities, you regularly encounter obstacles and hazards. In order to guarantee your achievement, one can acquire the skills to safeguard oneself from the barrage of pessimistic thoughts and deeds. It is imperative to not only maintain a dynamic and positive mindset, but also to exercise caution and awareness in order to prevent oneself from being exposed to detrimental individuals and circumstances that may posses intrusive negative influences. The utmost safeguard against these circumstances will be derived from fostering a profound sense of affection and empathy.

At every instant, an ongoing conflict occurs between superior and inferior forces across the globe. An arena in which this struggle may manifest itself is located within the realm of the human psyche. Individuals are often unwitting vessels for the thoughts and desires of others, absorbing their energy in a manner that is frequently internalized. These musings are akin to electrical conductions: imperceptible to the eye, yet palpable to the senses and manifesting tangible consequences.

These contemplations have the potential to impinge upon the caliber of your leadership. Due to your elevated position, a substantial number of individuals will direct their thoughts and exert their efforts towards you. Certain individuals may seek to assign blame to you as a means of deflecting attention from their own disruptions, while others may view you with an envious disposition. Furthermore, certain individuals may merely seek to evaluate your abilities. In the absence of an ample internal reservoir of affection, you will find yourself bereft of the essential fortification required to shield against the ceaseless onslaught of adverse energies. Nevertheless, profound inner affection will enable you to deflect such detrimental energy, or even to alchemize it in a manner that nullifies any deleterious consequences. Hence, it is essential to consistently establish an emotional guard of compassion as a means of safeguarding oneself, while bearing in mind that in order to extend love to others, it is imperative to first cultivate self-love.

Love as Relationship

Simultaneously, it is important to bear in mind that it is expected of you to exhibit love towards your fellow individuals. This point is underscored by all of the predominant religions across the globe:

Brahmanism: Abstain from treating others in a manner that would inflict suffering upon oneself.

Buddhism: Abstain from causing harm to others in manners that you, yourself, might deem hurtful.

Christianity espouses the principle of treating others in a manner that aligns with the way one desires to be treated.

In the religion of Islam, one cannot be considered a truly devout believer until one exhibits a sincere desire for their fellow brethren to attain the same aspirations and benefits that they seek for themselves.

Judaism teaches the principle of refrainment from imposing upon others that which one finds detestable.

Zoroastrianism postulates that only the actions considered beneficial to oneself should be done, without causing harm to others.

In the philosophy of Taoism, it is incumbent upon individuals to consistently view the well-being of their neighbor as their own gain and consider their neighbor's detriment as their own loss.

While the injunction to extend love towards one's fellow human beings in the same manner as oneself holds true universally, a limited number of individuals have the capacity to adhere to it. Indeed, it is a rarity to encounter individuals who even endeavor to do so. Nevertheless, as an individual in a position of leadership, it is within your capacity to transcend ordinary moral constraints. Truly, it is inadequate to solely have an affection for your fellow human beings that is equal to the love you have for yourself. Indeed, it is possible to develop an even greater sense of affection towards those individuals for whom one bears responsibility, surpassing the love one has for oneself.

As a leader, view yourself as the custodian of those under your guidance rather than the owner, conducting yourself as you would when entrusted with a valuable asset. This methodology promotes the recognition of the God-like essence within each individual and positions oneself as a representative of the divine assigned to cultivate the God-like essence within others. Engaging in this form of service to God embodies love at its highest level.

To revisit the previously mentioned analogy of a mother and child, it can be observed that the intensity of their affection derives from its inherent purity. The mother's love for her child extends beyond mere affection and encompasses a deep care and concern comparable to the love she has for herself. She perceives that child as vulnerable, acknowledging that without her assistance, the child could potentially suffer from hunger or even perish. Put differently, the mother holds the belief that her child's existence is reliant upon her, and as a result, she dedicates an immense amount of care, reverence, and focus to their bond. In the same fashion that a mother surpasses the midpoint to ensure the welfare of her child, you have the capacity to exude a comparable level of affection in order to prosper in your role as a leader. You are entrusted with the role of a guardian with the primary objective of fostering a tranquil and cooperative state of being for all individuals. In the realm of material existence, this particular form of affection is recognized as maternal or paternal love, representing a pinnacle of human expression towards the Divine.

Frequently, individuals perceive God as a being deserving of profound admiration, trepidation, and veneration. Nevertheless, this is a rudimentary observation. There exist numerous alternative forms of potential relationships with the divine. An individual whose affection deepens acknowledges the capacity to embrace a relationship with God not only as the

Divine Creator, but also as a confidant or as a cherished offspring. Whilst the bond of friendship is indeed deep, as it signifies the affection between two individuals of comparable standing, the filial connection holds even greater significance as the caregiver acts in the best interest of the more vulnerable party. This statement appears to be paradoxical, as it goes against the notion that God consistently holds a position of superiority. Nevertheless, through divine arrangement, it is conceivable to establish such a connection within the realms of altruistic love.

In this elevated state of divine awareness, an individual has the ability to devote themselves to the service of God while fulfilling the responsibilities of a parental figure, wherein God assumes the role of the child. This profound love demonstrates an unwavering commitment to providing safeguard and support, accompanied by meticulous attention and unwavering devotion. If you strive to harness the utmost benevolence in your capacity as a leader, it is imperative that you cultivate a profound appreciation for this magnitude of affection.

An exemplary illustration substantiating this proposition is derived from the work of Charles Darwin. As explicitly documented in his memoir, Darwin engaged in regular promenades along the designated pathway known as the "sandwalk" adjacent to his residence. This practice held significance beyond his physical well-being. It constituted a crucial element of his intellectual regimen. While engaged in the act of walking, a multitude of his perplexing enigmas were successfully solved. Darwin referred to his "sandwalk" as his "contemplation trail." More recently, Michael Mangum, the esteemed president and CEO of the Mangum Group, expressed a similar sentiment when he stated,

I am of the conviction that physical fitness significantly influences my job performance. I typically engage in physical activity in the midday hours, generally between the hours of one to four in the afternoon. I have observed a noticeable increase in my overall energy levels upon returning from a physical exercise session. Moreover, I observe that by opting to engage in physical activity during daylight hours, my mind naturally gravitates towards work-related matters while I am in motion. I experience heightened levels of creativity during physical exercise."

A scientific experiment has been conducted to examine the potential for the act of engaging in physical activity to generate innovative ideas. At Stanford University, two psychologists, Marily Oppezzo and Daniel Schwartz, conducted a study where participants were instructed to generate as many alternative applications for a given object as they could within a time limit of four minutes. The test has been discovered to be indicative of individuals' level of creativity in both their professional and personal lives. An instance in this experiment entailed a participant's association of the word "button" with concepts such as a miniature doorknob, a doll's eye, a small sieve, and a trail marker. Oppezzo and Schwartz observed that, on average, participants generated six original alternative applications for a given set of stimuli while situated in a confined chamber, directly in front of a featureless surface. Astoundingly, whilst maintaining a leisurely stride on a treadmill and directing their attention towards a static wall, they managed to conceive of ten innovative applications for an additional battery of examinations. It indicates that individuals exhibit superior creativity while in motion as opposed to being stationary. This observation was validated through the utilization of an alternative creativity assessment, wherein participants were evaluated based on their capability to formulate unique analogies for the purpose of encapsulating intricate concepts. When considering the phenomenon of a "light bulb blowing out," individuals may associate it with the concept of "vomiting while consuming liquid." Similarly, when contemplating a "budding cocoon," individuals may envision the act of "emerging from a meditation retreat." Oppezzo and Schwartz's research has revealed that engaging in a walking activity on a treadmill, as opposed to being stationary, enhances the generation of superior analogies. Furthermore, this advantageous impact endures even after the walking session concludes.

In a subsequent study, Oppezzo and Schwartz instructed participants to undertake these two assessments either in a stationary-seated state or a mobile-seated state. Namely, during the initial session, the subjects underwent the tests while either seated or engaging in ambulation on a treadmill. In contrast, during the subsequent session, all subjects conducted the tests exclusively in a seated position. Oppezzo and Schwartz observed that following the act of walking during the initial session, participants displayed significantly deteriorated performance when assuming a seated position for the subsequent session. Nevertheless, they excelled in comparison to individuals who took part in both sessions. This implies that the positive impact of walking on creativity perseveres beyond the completion of the walking activity, demonstrating that even a short duration of walking, such as four minutes, is effective.

Indeed, Oppezzo and Schwartz were not the initial pioneers to uncover the correlation between exercise and heightened creativity. Twenty years prior, a study conducted by Hannah Steinberg at Middlesex University had examined the impact of aerobic exercise on individuals' subsequent creative cognition. Steinberg requested participants to generate a multitude of alternative applications for the tin can, either following a vigorous 25-minute aerobic exercise session or after viewing a neutral 25-minute documentary showcasing geological rock formations.

Steinberg discovered that individuals who engaged in an aerobic workout demonstrated a greater capacity for generating a varied range of responses when compared to individuals who simply viewed the video. Nevertheless, the experiment unveiled more than just that. Steinberg requested that the subjects regroup at the laboratory the following day. Participants who had engaged in the aerobic workout on the preceding day were instructed to observe the 25-minute video, whereas those who had watched the video the previous day were directed to perform 25 minutes of aerobic dance. Following the aforementioned manipulation, participants were subsequently instructed to reattempt the creative thinking test. However, their task was slightly modified, requiring them to generate as many alternative applications for a novel object, namely a cardboard box. On this particular occasion, individuals who engaged in a dance routine for a duration of 25 minutes demonstrated an inclination towards generating a wider range of responses. Collectively, these two days of experimentation indicate that engaging in aerobic exercise has a positive influence on subsequent cognitive creativity.

Based on these personal experiences and psychological studies, we can derive two key messages that can be taken away from this. Initially, it is imperative to acknowledge that the ideas generated during exercise, though seemingly random, possess a notable degree of order and coherence. Some are often creative. Carefully reconsider these options and evaluate their potential to offer innovative assistance.

Furthermore, it should be noted that even short durations of physical activity, such as a mere four-minute walk, serve to enhance subsequent creative thinking, thus presenting an opportunity for individuals to harness this advantageous effect. For example, engaging in short walks or engaging in other types of aerobic exercise prior to an interview or a meeting that demands innovative thinking and creativity may be advantageous, as long as it does not cause excessive fatigue beforehand.

One of the aspects that I greatly admire about Bruce Beatty is his knack for distilling complex matters down to their fundamental core. For instance, Bruce conveyed to me, "One of the most rudimentary interpretations of management that I have ever come across is 'accomplishing tasks by means of utilizing the efforts of others.'"

That not only serves as an excellent elucidation of management, but it also enlightens one about the most favorable point of origin when contemplating the establishment of a team to assume leadership roles: commencing with the individuals involved.

An Existing Team

Assuming leadership of an established team necessitates a tactful approach, a realization I acquired not just from my experience at Kinko's, but also through various other roles. The practice of modesty can have a significant impact. This is a principle that Bruce claims to have acquired during his childhood while encountering unfamiliar circumstances due to frequent relocations within his family. "I came to realize that being the most intelligent individual in the class did not necessarily equate to the utmost advantage," he expresses. Therefore, it is advisable to heed the insights of individuals who are actively engaged in the tasks at hand. When transitioning to a new department within various professional environments, upon receiving proper introductions and establishing my authoritative role, I would dedicate the initial two to three weeks to personally collaborating with each employee, offering my assistance in the execution of their responsibilities. In order to effectively oversee that individual, it was imperative for me to gain comprehension of their profession, ascertain their motivations, and equip them with the necessary resources for fulfilling their responsibilities."

Bruce further highlights the constraints associated with the individual in comparison to a collective entity. When one assumes the role of a manager, it entails a minimum of eight hours of work. One could potentially dedicate a considerable amount of time, specifically 16 hours per day, in order to fulfill the responsibilities of both their own job as well as that of another individual. It is possible to opt for a relentless work schedule of working round the clock, taking on the workload equivalent to three individuals. Subsequently, could you surmise the outcome? It's physically impossible. It is necessary to accomplish it by means of intermediary individuals. It is imperative that you attend to the individuals responsible for the task at hand. They have the capability to either enhance or diminish your reputation." He proceeds to provide insightful guidance that I believe every Essential Leader should bear in consideration regarding the individuals comprising their team: "I have always held the belief that people do not work under my authority. I am not employed by individuals. I work with people. Their triumph equates to my triumph. Their shortcomings reflect upon my own inadequacies."

Hire Well

After attaining a solid grounding within an established team, there may arise a circumstance wherein you have the prospect to recruit individuals of your choice. Ideally, the manifestation of this outcome stems from expansion, yet it may also be attributable to employee attrition.

A leader of utmost significance comprehends the essentiality of fostering a team comprising a distinctive range of competencies. Skills serve as the fundamental basis of your exploration and development. An essential leader not only recruits individuals who complement the skills of their team, but also continually evaluates the team to identify any skill deficiencies. Why the latter? As a result of (1) the inevitable turnover of personnel and (2) the dynamic nature of markets, there may be a need for individuals with fresh skill sets.

In the book Traction, authored by Gino Wickman, the concept of "Right Person, Right Seat" is discussed. Wickman emphasizes the importance of continuously evaluating whether an individual is the suitable fit for a particular role. Specifically, he advises asking oneself if the person is indeed the right fit, and if so, ensuring they are positioned in a role that optimizes their potential for success and contributes the most value to the organization.

It is advisable to conduct periodic evaluations of your team in order to gain insights into any potential areas of deficiency within your team. However, a Leader of Utmost Importance comprehends that disparities differ based on the position, the organization, the sector, and so forth. Most assuredly, the primary consideration that comes to mind for the majority of individuals is the notion of skill gaps. When inquiring with the personnel regarding the issue of addressing deficiencies, they contemplate, "I possess individuals with commendable proficiency in a certain skill, yet their competence in another area is subpar, and furthermore, we lack the necessary expertise in a third area."

In terms of the industry you are involved in, you have the ability to take a more expansive approach in this regard. Upon observing your team, it becomes evident that there are a number of highly skilled and expressive individuals who possess exceptional communication abilities, particularly in the domain of sales. They establish excellent rapport with clients. However, their attention to detail falls short." As a consequence, though you successfully generate significant business and foster strong connections, you encounter challenges in effectively executing tasks. Therefore, it may be advantageous for you to cultivate or employ individuals who possess exemplary organizational skills and a strong focus on completing assigned tasks. This endeavor will enable you to achieve a greater equilibrium within your team's composition.

You may have observed that the concept of evaluating discrepancies within your team aligns with your own introspection as a leader. You aspire to cultivate a harmonious and versatile leadership presence, just as you seek to foster a harmonious and versatile collective dynamic within your team. However, it is unfortunate that hiring is frequently overlooked as a critical component in fostering a thriving team and organization, despite its pivotal role in the formation of exceptional teams. As a noteworthy leader, your emphasis ought to lie in selecting candidates whom you anticipate will evolve into invaluable leaders as well. I cannot emphasize sufficiently the significance of commencing the exploration by precisely outlining

"The vacancy you are looking to hire for, "The employment opportunity you wish to fill, "The role you are seeking to staff, "The position you are aiming to appoint a candidate to,

the methodology you will employ to evaluate potential candidates, and

Defining the manifestation of success post the successful onboarding of the new individual.

Initially, prioritize the development of a concise enumeration of essential proficiencies and qualifications, which ought to encompass competencies that are not readily acquirable through instruction. Subsequently, generate a secondary inventory denoting desirable proficiencies and qualifications. Please thoroughly evaluate and revise the aforementioned lists to attain the highest level of precision possible, as they will serve as a crucial reference for your decision-making process. To clarify, no item should be included in your list of essentials unless it is absolutely nonnegotiable. As an illustration, it is advisable not to include "four year degree" in the list of requirements in the event that you are open to hiring a candidate with substantial work experience that compensates for the absence of a college degree, as determined by your assessment. If you are open to considering individuals who satisfy either criterion, it is recommended to prioritize the inclusion of a four-year degree experience in the preferred category rather than the mandatory category. Alternatively, one might encounter a scenario where the required qualifications include "two years of prior business experience," while the preferred qualifications entail "a range of three to five years of prior business experience."

Please bear in mind that your objective is to recruit individuals who have the potential to become exceptional leaders in the future, not necessarily at present. Just as one may not have considered themselves a leader prior to assuming the role, it is imperative to acknowledge that prospective team members may not even perceive themselves as suitable candidates for the position. It is possible that they may have a deficiency in self-assurance regarding their own skills, thereby hindering their ability to acknowledge their potential for achievement in the given position. It is incumbent upon you to assist them in recognizing their inherent capabilities.

Now presents an optimal occasion to thoroughly examine the content in this book and establish a set of overarching attributes that are essential for an effective leader. These qualities can then serve as a criterion for assessing potential candidates during the hiring process. Subsequently, structure your recruitment procedure in accordance with the aforementioned criteria by posing inquiries that enable you to assess the potential of candidates in cultivating those crucial attributes.

It is important to bear in mind that leaders are shaped through nurture rather than innate abilities. Incorporating fresh talent presents a valuable occasion for a seasoned leader like yourself to nurture and cultivate a nascent team, molding them into formidable leaders with pronounced indispensability.

Please consider that coaching and development initiatives can contribute to the cultivation of robust leadership abilities, whereas cultural compatibility and empathy are more challenging to instill through conventional methods. These qualities should be evaluated and prioritized when making hiring decisions. I am unable to ascertain any training that could sufficiently align an individual with your company's ethos and team dynamics. If during the interview process, they demonstrate a lack of suitability, it is highly likely that they will continue to be unsuitable even after you have made the decision to employ them.

Selecting the appropriate individual significantly heightens the importance of evaluating their soft skills and compatibility with the company's culture prior to making a hiring decision. Please be aware that you will not always achieve perfection. There will be instances where an individual appears suitable or perhaps you have chosen to grant them an opportunity, only to discover that they are ultimately unsuitable. Utilize the knowledge acquired from these experiences to consistently refine your recruitment procedures in order to ensure future achievements.

As an essential leader, however, you possess the capacity to formulate a recruitment procedure that not only assesses a candidate's professional background, but also evaluates their compatibility with your team. The procedure will differ depending on the role being filled, the specific industry, the prevailing company culture, the scale of the organization, and the existing workforce composition. All of those factors will impact the decision-making process you select.

As an illustration, let us contemplate a substantial and well-established business in the service industry seeking to fill a senior role that involves direct interaction with discerning clientele. The procedure you employ may entail an initial assessment of resumes and subsequent evaluation using the aforementioned criteria. This would be followed by a pre-screening call, a face-to-face meeting with the hiring manager, and an interview day in which the candidate interacts with team members with whom they will potentially work. Subsequently, a job offer may be extended. During this progression, the pool of candidates is undergoing a distillation process, while soliciting and appraising feedback from all individuals who interact with the candidate. The entirety of the schedule provides you with the chance to ascertain the crucial alignment with the organizational culture.

On the other hand, in stark contrast, a small-scale enterprise seeking to hire a front-office personnel may engage in a significantly abbreviated selection process, typically necessitating a solitary interview session prior to extending a job offer.

Essential leaders assess every situation and devise hiring procedures that align with their requirements. They adopt a non-uniform approach, acknowledging the need to customize their strategies in order to identify the most suitable candidates for their vacant positions.

The ultimate phase of the recruitment process, particularly for exceptionally critical leaders, entails a dedicated emphasis on addressing the aforementioned deficiencies. Acquiring a capable new hire is the optimal strategy to address any deficiencies in your team's expertise, thereby ensuring the utmost quality of work from your team.

That final step is the reason behind my insistence on commencing the hiring procedures by meticulously elucidating the specific role you aim to occupy. I designate the process as "a sequence of actions." Commence by pondering upon two inquiries: "For what reason am I engaging in recruitment activities, and what tasks must be accomplished?" These responses serve as the most expeditious means to ascertain the specific requirements of the role and the necessities of your team. Upon attaining this level of clarity, your chances of selecting a candidate who embodies a broad range of experiences and perspectives, thereby complementing your team's existing deficiencies, will increase substantially. Bruce articulates it concisely when he states, "I believe the most effective leaders are those who strategically assemble a team of individuals who possess strengths that complement the leader's and organization's areas of weakness."

Based on my personal experience, I am confident in my aptitude for various facets of leadership and the effective management of daily operations. As a human being, I tend to harbor the conviction that I possess the correct solutions in numerous instances. From a rational standpoint, it follows that I would derive great satisfaction from collaborating with individuals who possess similar characteristics and qualities as myself. It is highly conceivable that we would establish a splendid rapport. However, the employment of a multitude of replicas of my own self would undoubtedly prove counterproductive, leading to a significant curtailment of advancement for both my team and my organization, as well as impeding personal growth. Alternatively, when seeking to expand my team, I initially evaluate the competencies and attributes of the existing members. As an imperative leader, it is my objective to recruit individuals who encourage the team to strive for improvement while ensuring that their presence does not impede the achievements of the team or the established culture. That's a tall order. Once successfully achieved, however, it yields significant benefits for the team, the organization, and the individual in a leadership role. It guarantees that not only will the team produce an enhanced work output, but also that team members will experience personal growth through the exchange of perspectives, engaging in discussions, and even engaging in constructive debates.

www.ingramcontent.com/pod-product-compliance
Lightning Source LLC
Chambersburg PA
CBHW050239120526
44590CB00016B/2158